Printed
For
Quixote Press
by
Ottumwa Printing, Inc.
105 South Birch
Ottumwa, Iowa 52501
515-682-2935

101 WAYS
TO
USE A DEAD RIVER FLY

by

Bruce Carlson

QUIXOTE PRESS
R.R. #4, Box 33B
Blvd. Station
Sioux City, Iowa
51109

QUIXOTE PRESS
Bruce Carlson
R.R. #4, Box 33B
Blvd. Station
Sioux City, Iowa
51109

PRINTED
IN
U.S.A.

v

The reader must appreciate the fact that none of these stories have ever been published before. Some of them could cause embarrassment to living people today. Because of that, some of the stories use fictitious names. In those cases, it should be understood that any similarity between those names and actual people, living or dead, is purely coincidental.

DEDICATION

This book is fondly dedicated to those little critters that come out of our rivers here in the Midwest. They are called a lot of things, but usually river flies.

TABLE OF CONTENTS

FOREWORD

101 WAYS TO USE A DEAD RIVER FLY will undoubtedly prove to be the 20th Century's most definitive work on the subject.

We are all a little richer for Bruce Carlson having the forsight.......foresite.......fosite.......vision to see a void in our body of knowledge about river flies and to do something about it.

Inof Splist
Literary Review Office
Journal of the Party Line
Prilspe, Hungary

PREFACE

The river fly that comes up our of our rivers here in the Midwest is certainly living proof of the value of good press and the disadvantage suffered by those without it.

The river fly is universally disliked, or worse. For a critter that doesn't bite, sting, kick or try to sell you new house siding, it certainly doesn't deserve that fate.

This book attempts to illustrate the value and usefulness of the river fly by listing 101 uses for that humble creature.

TECHNIQUE #1

SHOE DEODORIZER

 e have all had the unpleasant experience of finding that one of our pairs of shoes has developed an objectionable odor.

Perhaps that problem is due to the uppers not being of a material that allows the shoe to "breathe". Perhaps it can be traced to our failure to let a pair rest a bit between wearings.

Whatever the cause, the problem is not one that is pleasant to have. Nor is it a problem that has proven to one that is easy to solve.

That is, it hasn't been easy to solve up until now. Thanks to the river fly, a solution is at hand.

15

This business of shoes developing an offensive odor can be nipped in the bud. When the odor is first noticed, one need only to sprinkle a few dead river flies into the shoes prior to putting them on.

Immediately after putting the flies in the shoes, one should walk around in them for a few minutes in order to release all the benefits of the little critters.

Not only will the locker room odor be completely masked by that of the river flies, but that original odor will be sorely missed by your friends and neighbors.

TECHNIQUE #9

POTATO SALAD GARNISH

 n this world of uses for dead river flies, one of the most attractive uses is that as a garnish for potato salad.

It is necessary for us to avoid being overly rigid in our definition of what constitutes a dead river fly. For this purpose, we have to include those flying-around-type of river flies. Well, actually, it's really only the flying-around-type that will work for this one.

Pound for pound, there aren't a whole lot of things in this old world that taste better than potato salad. It's just one all 'round good thing to eat.

P.S. does, however, suffer one significant

disadvantage. It just plain looks washed out and tired. I mean, once you get by the white and the yellow, whatcha got?....not much.

And, that's where garnish comes in. A little garnish goes a long way toward making potato salad lood as good as it tastes.

Some river flies fetchingly decorating a potato salad just do all sorts of good things toward making it look a lot more exciting and appetizing.

The interesting contrasts in color between the whites and yellows of P.S. and the earthy tones of the river fly makes it a much more attractive dish to put on the table.

It is especially fetching if the river flies can be convinced to sit there and repeatedly open and close their wings. It sort of makes it a potato salad mobile, as it were.

Notwithstanding how pretty such a thing can be,

the real advantage of the river flies as garnish for potato salad is obvious when one goes to remove the garnish from the salad.

The grateful cook finds that he/she doesn't have to laboriously pick a bunch of parsley springs or something else out of the salad. All that's necessary is to wave a large spoon or towel over the salad, and the garnish will fly away on its own.

How much handier can you get than that. Why, parsley garnish, even at its best, can't do that. It just sits there like it didn't have a brain at all.

I'd appreciate it a whole lot if you'd tell your friends that you heard it here first.

TECHNIQUE #14

INSULATION FOR BUILDINGS

 ith an R factor of somewhere between Q and S, it is obvious that river flies make very good insulation.

The little critters can be gathered up and blown into the wall as you would any ohter traditional "blow-in insulation."

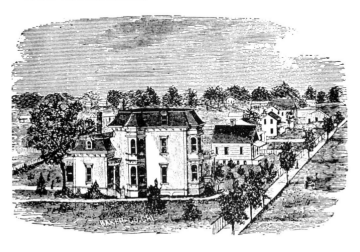

A few hundred pounds of river flies is all it takes to fully insulate the average three-bedroom home.

Of course, it will take a bit more if you are going to get fussy and want a home with other features such as bathrooms, living room, kitchen, and so

forth. In this latter case, you might want to as much as double the recommended amount of insulation.

Of the various characteristics that the home-owner should possess, one of the more useful ones were he to use this type of insulation is that he should have a rather pronounced tolerance for the smell of river flies.

TECHNIQUE #22

THE COSMETIC DETRACTOR

ll the salves and creams eventually prove to be of no effect. All the rubs, sprays and facial exercises end up being to no avail.

In the end, the little wrinkles on your neck and the little crow's feet around your eyes will have their way.

That is, all that was true before the discovery of the wonders of dead river flies. No longer need we wage a losing battle with the various preparations available from your friendly druggist.

The hours grow short for those persisteant little wrinkles around the neck and those heretofore inescapable crow's feet around your eyes. Youth, borne on the wings of the river fly, rises from the ashes of age.

All that's necessary is one well-formed river fly, sound of limb. The river fly serves as a decoy or a detractor.... to draw the attention of the observer from those wrinkles.

Say, for example, you have some of those fetching little crow feet lines near your eyes and you don't want your date to notice them. All you have to do is to hang the aforementioned river fly from the end of your nose or the pointy part of your chin.

That big old critter hanging there will go a long ways toward distracting your date's eyes from the offending wrinkles.

Those ocassional pesky gray hairs that violate your otherwise youthful head of hair can be made to all but disappear from the eyes of the beholder

if a river fly is gaily perched on your left cheek....
kind of a beauty spot, don't you know.

And, a river fly sticking out of each of your ears
will seem to make that little mole on your chin all
but disappear.

Conversely, if you happen to have naturally
occuring river flies sticking out of your ears, the
attention of your loved one can be diverted from
those by hanging a real mole (as in gopher) from
your chin.

I know this isn't
a good represent-
ation of a mole,
but it's the clos-
est I can find
this morning.

But all that is going a bit afield from the subject of
this book. Such things are discussed fully in a
companion book: 101 THINGS TO DO WITH A
DEAD MOLE.

TECHNIQUE #28

AS A LOVE
POTION

he lowly river fly proves to be the answer to that age-old search for a love potion.

Yes, gentle reader, even a love potion.

What seems to be endless applications for dead river flies even includes this, the dream of

alchemists of old.

Unlike others, this love potion does not depend on physiological effects. Because of that, it is all the more insidious.

While the love potionee might steel him or herself for a traditional physiological effect of the dead river fly, this lowly little creature has other cards to play.

What the love potioner does, at what seems to be an opportune moment, is to simply take a handful of dead river flies out of his/her pocket/purse and pitch them right up in the air.

Said river files will, of course, come raining back down, cleverly engaging in the love potionee's clothing, hair, ears, and so forth.

The secret to this whole thing is that while the love potionee's attention is thus diverted, the love potioner can gain control of the situation.

At this point, the love potioner makes his/her move. Notwithstanding the fact that the potionee is not affected psysiologically, that person is caught with his/her defenses down. . . . . . . that is to say, they are more of less defenseless.

With that kind of distraction, things just sort of happen, don't you know.

TECHNIQUE #37

RIVER FLIES ON A
CHECKERBOARD

or this application, simply take an ordinary checkerboard such as from a game of checkers or a chess set.

On alternating squares, put a small to medium-sized blob of glue.

While the glue is wet yet yet yet wet still moist, place one dead river fly on each of the glue spots.

After the glue is well-cured, you will then have a checkerboard with alternating squares containing a dead river fly.

Now, I haven't the foggiest idea of what you can do with such a thing, but if you ever needed a checkerboard with alternating squares contain-

ing a dead river fly, you'll have one ready to go.
And, all those other folks won't.

TECHNIQUE #46

A REMINDER OF
GOOD TIMES

 hose folks who have taken a vacation to one of the prime river fly areas of America's great Midwest might well want to avail themselves of a really great way to recall their vacation.

A really nice way to do this is to make your own mattress that you have filled with dead river flies.

This can, of course, take one gosh-awful number of those expired little critters, but the results are really worth the effort.

When the farsighted vacationeer from areas devoid of river flies comes home from his vacation and is the proud possessor of several bushels of dead river flies, he has the makings of one fine souvenir. He can stuff all those flies into a bag-like thing so he can fit it right on top of the existing mattress on his bed.

A night spent on this mattress will bring back countless memories of that vacation out in the land of river flies.

This mattress is, of course, unique in lots of ways. One of the more pleasant ones is that it even has its own sound. As one rolls about in his bed at night, the squishing of the dried-out little bodies will so clearly remind one of that vacation. It's a little bit like the mood music tapes that you can buy, you know, the ones with crashing waves, babbling brooks, and so forth.

TECHNIQUE #51

AND PILLOWS, TOO

his techniques #51 is much like the last one in that it involves filling a bed accessory with dead river flies.

This time, however, it's a pillow that can be stuffed with those little critters.

A pillow stuffed with river flies takes a whole lot fewer of them than does a mattress. This can be an advantage if baggage space is a problem in bringing things home.

Like with the mattress, the pillow will bring that vacation back to mind through the sounds of those little carcasses crunching through the night.

One difficulty that a person can encounter with either the mattress (see technique 46) or the pillow is that these devices will sometimes tend to migrate toward a light.

TECHNIQUE #55

A MEANS TO IM-
PART A FISHY SMELL
TO DRAPES & CURTAINS

his recommended technique for imparting a fishy smell to your drapes or curtains is really quite simple. All you have to do is to scoop up a generous handful of dead river flies and moisten them down with clear tapwater until the resulting mass is a mess.

Firmly press the wad of wet soggy river flies onto the drape or curtain with even pressure. The wet wad should be

held on to the fabric until the opposite side shows evidence of the moisture having migrated through.

For detailed information as to why one would want to have fishy smelling drapes or curtains, the reader is advised to purchase at least one copy of 101 WAYS TO USE FISHY SMELLING DRAPES OR CURTAINS, by Bruce Carlson, 162 pp, QUIXOTE PRESS, 1991.

For your convenience, an order form for that book can be found on page 62 of this volume.

TECHNIQUE #62

USING A RIVER FLY
TO MEET GIRLS

 tricktly speaking, this particular technique for using a dead river fly isn't what you'd call super exact since you need a live river fly to do the job.

But since even live river flies are gonna be dead ones within a very few hours anyway, we can, for all practical purposes, consider all river flies to be dead ones.

River flies are an ideal way to meet girls. All you have to do is to keep a sharp eye on a good lookin' girl until a river fly lands on her. At that point, the careful observer can rush up to said girl and solicitiously brush the offending creature off her.

The location of the fly on the girl can have a profound impact, of course, on the reaction that the brusher will get from the brushee. Some pretty serious mistakes have been made in that department.

It would not be appropriate in this here family publication to go into just a whole lot of detail regarding the most advantageous locations on a girl for the fly to land. If a fellow can't figure all that out for himself, he has no business being out late enough at night to see river flies anyway.

TECHNIQUE #68

TELLIN' TIME

 ou can tell time using a dead river fly by using the twin principles of gravitational attraction and micro-atomicsynthesis.

All you gotta do is to find a dead river fly hanging on a wall, a light pole, or some of other convenient vertical surface.

You can carefully dislodge the river fly with some sort of prodding tool. A reasonably priced and

ordinary kitchen spoon has proven to be an effective instrument for this.

If you carefully dislodge the river fly with the aforementioned tool, you can easily see which

41

direction it falls. This tells you immediately which way is down.

Then you need only to quickly turn to the left, do a quarter turn in either direction, follow this with a reverse half gainer, and simuitaneiusly extend your left arm fully away from your body.

Your left arm will then be pointing due north. And, once you know which way is north, you can

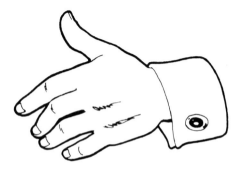

figure the time from the direction that shadows are cast from vertical objects.

Some folks like to sort of simplify things by using the same vertical surface for shadow determination that they orginally pried the river fly from. The novice, of course, need not concern himself with such nicities as that.

Repeated executions of this procedure have demonstrated that it is an accurate means of determining the time of day.

Finding out the time of night is a little bit of a triekier.....trickke.....trickter.....harder thing to do since the sun doesn't cast very good shadows at night. But, then, of course, sometimes we have to stand back and examine our lives. Sometimes we have to ask ourselves why we're staying out so late at night that we've lost track of time.

TECHNIQUE #74

LIP BOMB BE AM
BAL ME B....GOO

ou know how aggravating cold sores can be. They don't often hurt just a real whole lot, but when they do, they can hurt like all get out. Even when they don't really hurt, they are a terrible bother.

And, just about the time you think you have the dang thing on the run, you inadvertently lick the

silly thing. Then you're back to square one again, and have to outlive the cold sore all over again.

All that inconvenience and aggravation need no longer plague the serious student of means of using dead river flies. An old home remedy using river flies provides an end to the cold sore foolishness.

All you have to do is to make a paste, using ground-up river flies and a little bit of a good quality corn oil.

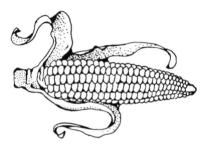

Put a handful of the dead river flies in a blender with one-and-a-half tablespoons of the corn oil and turn on to "Mix" or "Blend".

A few seconds of that and you will be rewarded with a nice batch of a good thick puree made of river flies and corn oil.

This soothing paste of homogenized river flies and corn oil can be applied to the cold sore.

The river fly doesn't really have any real curative power in itself, but it really does a bang up job of keeping a person from licking his lips.

TECHNIQUE #79

THE EXTENDER

ometimes in the hustle and bustle of our busy lives we tend to forget our little furred and feathered friends. We tend to think about people's needs and sometimes forget those of creatures that simply stand and serve (or more usually, lay around and serve.)

As we consider the many and varied uses for dead river flies, we should remember those that

benefit our pets, those that make life a little more pleasant for those important little creatures in our lives.

And, an important one is the usefulness of dead river flies as extenders for cat food. We've all heard of Hamburger Helper. Well, river flies make good filler for pet foods.

Perhaps your cat or even your dog lacks a little zing in his life. Maybe a little gastonomic kick will make your pet a happier one.

And, remember, a happy pet makes a happy home.

TECHNIQUE #81

GASOLINE MILEAGE
EXTENDER

he economic advantage of affecting dramatic increases in the gas mileage of your automobile is one of the most attractive benefits of this book. Even if you drive only six thousand miles a year, if you were to double the mileage, you could save up to $500.00 per year.

Annual savings of even that modest $500.00 certainly illustrates the usefulness of this book and the economic savvy exhibited by he or she who bought it.

 Now, you must understand, of course, that I don't exactly know how to use dead river flies to extend the mileage of your car, but, after all, I can't do everything:: You need to take some responsibility for these things, too, you know. A little responsibility here, a little responsibility there, and pretty soon you'll be a good citizen.

TECHNIQUE #84

GARDEN FERTILIZER

iver flies have been scientifically and indisputedly proven to be about average as a garden fertilizer. Apparently they have quite a bit of iron, phosphorous, and other such goodies that plants like.

Unlike lots of kinds of fertilizer, you don't have to bring river fly fertilizer to the garden, it more or

less brings itself. This alone is a real advantage to the gardener.

All that is necessary to attract the river flies to

your garden is to string a line of lights along each row of the garden. For this, Christmas tree lights have been proven to be especially convenient.

Some of the finest gardens here in the Midwest are those that have been the grateful beneficiaries of river fly fertilizer.

Those folks who have the greatest opportunity to take advantage of this flying fertilizer are those that live on houseboats. The proximity of the river flies to those folks makes this an especially attractive alternative to traditional fertilizers. And, those who live on houseboats and complain about not having enough room for a garden are just natural born whiners.

TECHNIQUE #88

DENTAL FLOSS

t should be emphasized that one should not attempt to use the entire creature as a flossing material. It is only the long trailin' thingies that the river fly trails behind him as he flies that makes for good flossing material. The scientific name for these long trailin' thingies is "long trailin' thingies."

This particular application is one that is best used with relatively large river flies. The smaller ones have those long trailin' thingies too short for convenient gripping for normal use.

The diligent user of dental floss should be aware of the danger of using flossing as an alternative to proper brushing. The use of even especially effective flosses such as river fly "long trailin' thingies"

does not take the place of regular brushing/. every now and then.

Another advantage of the use of river fly long trailin' thingies is that the fishy flavor of the river fly will effectively mask the objectionable after-taste of toothpaste.

TECHNIQUE #89

IS IT OFF?

he one problem that has plagued mankind since the dawn of time has been the nagging question that eventually comes to roost on the subconscious of each and every one of us.

DOES THE LITTLE LIGHT IN THE REFRIGERATOR REALLY, REALLY GO OFF WHEN YOU CLOSE THE DOOR?

There are those among us who will argue the issue with various degrees of enthusiasm and conviction, but how many of us really know?

I don't mean to ask how many of us "know" in some theoretical or abstract sense. I mean "How man of us really KNOW, and KNOW about our own refrigerator in our own home?

It's like Mt. Vesuvius, or St. Helens, or wherever it was.....the question is just there.

Well, I can tell you from first-hand experience that it isn't a particularly good idea to stick a cat in there for a few minutes to then see how big the pupils of the critter's eyes are after that time.

In theory, of course, it sounds great. If the cat's pupils are really big, it's 'cause the inside of the refrig was dark. If the pupils are real little, it means it was well lit in there while the door was closed.

But, theory and practice can lead vastly different lives. I won't go into all the awful details of just what happened, but I can assure you it was a pretty ugly affair. I don't 'spose that one person out of a hundred knows how much damage a panicky cat can do to the inside of a refrigerator.

And I don't 'spose that most folks know what a mother can do to a boy when she finds out what a panicky cat can do to the inside of a refrigerator.

River flies, though, are a whole 'nother story. So, what if a small covey of river flies do panic when they's locked in a refrigerator? What's a panicky little old river fly gonna do of any damage? Nothing, that's what he's gonna do, nothing at all.

But those little one hundredth of an ounce little flyin' tattletales will tell you exactly what went on in the refrig while the door was shut. If, when you open it again, the critters are all clustered around the light bulb, it was on while the door was shut. If they are all scattered around in a random pattern, that means the light was off.

I don't know if the little light goes off when you shut the door of your refrig. In fact, if you were just really, really honest with yourself, neither do you.

But, I sure know what's goin' on inside my refrigerator wattwise when I shut my door. When I pulled that little experiment with some river flies, I found 'em scattered in a perfectly random manner when I opened the door up.

Well, okay, there was that one kind of rowdy pair sitting on the broccolli necking, but I didn't figure that was of any statisical significance.

The important thing is that I can drop right off to sleep of a night now, not havin' to lay there wondering if the light in the refrigerator goes off when we shut the door.

TECHNIQUE #91

THE INVENTOR

t was just a matter of time until some enterprising inventor would come up with the idea of harnessing the incredible total power expended by the jillions of river flies that will congregate at one place along the river on a hot summer night.

And, that's just what Josh Abrams of the little
village of Wallford, Minnesota, did one summer
several years ago.

Josh's idea was really rather clever in that it pro-
vided a source of power throughout the nights
that the river flies were swarming.

The mechanism he developed consisted of pairs
of paddle-like devices mounted on poles near the
river. These paddles were such that they would
stick almost straight out from the pole until they

became loaded down with river flies. Then they would pivot down parallel to the pole. In the process, the paddles would slide past each other, wiping the flies off each of the opposing paddles.

Thus freed of the river flies, the paddle would immediately swing back up to the horizontal position, generating a little electricity in the process.

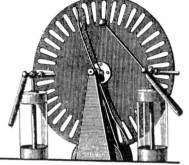

The constant swinging up and down of those paddles would generate enough electricity to run the lights needed to attract the river flies to the machine. On especially good nights, Josh would have enough electricity left over to operate a small radio.

The general consensus of opinion among the folks in Wallford was that Josh's device was a technical stroke of genius, even though it was a commercial flop.

I was just kidding you about the order form for 101 WAY TO USE FISHY SMELLING DRAPES OR CURTAINS back on page 38.

TECHNIQUE #92

A BIGGER BANG

nyone who has walked into a grassy area heavily laden with river flies knows full well how the air can suddenly turn brown with the thousands of little wings bearing the flies back into the air because of the disturbance. They often all seem to take flight at the same time.

This led an inventor, the name of whom is lost to us now, to come up with an idea that is preserved in some old drawings and notes found recently in an old house.

The invention is rather well documented in those notes and the drawings shown on the following page.

Time has faded the ink of the notes, but enough can be figured out to indicate that searching for uses for river flies is not something new.

63

The sketch on the left shows the traditional firearms cartridge of the time, with the traditional gun powder charge.

The drawing on the right shows a similar cartridge except it is filled with river flies instead

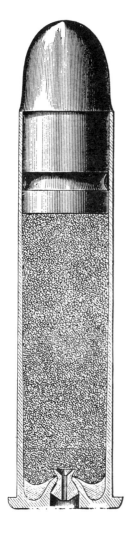

of gunpowder. The principle apparently was to agitate the little fellers all at once so they would all start fluttering their little wings at the same time. This simultaneous and sudden action would forcibly eject the bullet from the shell much as does the ignition of gunpowder.

The drawing on the right with the river flies clearly shows what the accompanying notes alluded to, in that the inventor was of the opinion that the river flies would be so much more effective than gunpowder that they would not only eject the bullet such as the one on the left, but would also send along the additional load of some smaller projectiles.

The careful reader might have, by this time, noted that I've taken some liberties with the system of numbering these techniques. What I've done is to eliminate those sort of ho-hum numbers in favor of the more exciting ones.

Take, for example, numbers 23 and 56. Those are about as ordianry as an old sock so I simply struck them from the system.

I know you'll be quietly appreciative of that, but there is no need to write and thank me. Just do a kind deed for someone else.

TECHNIQUE #93

MOSQUITO DECOY

ow, there are going to be some Doubting Thomases who aren't going to believe this one, but it does work.

I wouldn't have believed it myself, but we had a family outing some months ago where we tried it, and it worked like a charm.

What we did was use some dead river flies as mosquito decoys to scare away the real ones.

So, during one of those evenings of family togetherness when you all are sittin' around studying river flies, you might just make some special note of something. You might just compare how a river fly looks much like a large mosquito.

As you study them, you will find there are really only four easily identifiable differences in the appearance of these two critters.

(1) The river fly is much larger than his pesky little cousin.

(2) The mosquito has legs longer than the river fly in proportion to the size of the bodies.

(3) The river fly has those long trailin' thingies.

(4) The wings of the mosquito are narrower relative to its body size than are the wings of the river fly.

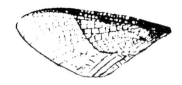

If it weren't for these significant differences, the river fly would look like a mosquito on steroids.

A little kitchen table surgery on half a dozen or so river flies can do wonders toward getting yourself that many critters that are the size of river flies, but look all in the world like mosquitos.

All you have to do is to:

(1) remove the long trailin' thingies, and then bend them into an approximation of a mosquito's leg

(2) glue the new "leg" onto the river fly

(3) carefully trim the wings down into

those in the shape of a mosquito
wing

In these three easy steps you have suddenly created some "mosquitos" the size of a small mouse.

Now, mosquitos aren't the smartest things in the world. In fact, they've been found to be just a little bit smarter than a wife-beater and just a little bit dumber than a dirty sock.

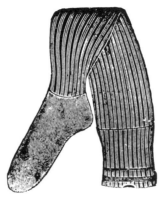

So, while the skeeter's intelligence isn't something to write home about, they are smart enough to know not to mess with another skeeter that's the size of a small mouse.

Now that you have your half dozen out doorsy bouncers, you can take them with you on your next outing. And, when you do, you'll be pleasantly surprised to find that the mosquitos will completely leave you alone. You can go to a lakeshore or even to a low-lying marshy area, and find yourself free of those pesky mosquitos.

If you're of a mind to, you can frolic around in your birthday suit, and not have to worry about mosquitos.

And, like I say, I know it works because I tried it a few months ago. The kids had just gotten new ice skates for Christmas, so they had to have an ice-skating party the very next day, of course.

I had the foresight to take my reconstructed river flies along so we wouldn't have to contend with mosquitos, of course.

And, it worked. We weren't bothered by those pesky little sketters all during the party.

TECHNIQUE #95

PORTABLE CHARCOAL

 nother little outdoorsy hint that the busy homemaker will find just handier than all get out is that you can use dead river flies as a BBQ charcoal substitute.

A good double handful of these little suckers kept handy in the glove compartment will often prove to be just what you need when you set up an impromptu picnic.

To facilitate lighting the dried-up river flies, it helps soak them down with a little used crankcase oil. That will start 'em out easily with one match.

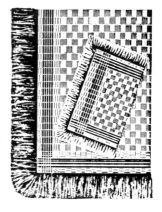

Now, we all know that gasoline, oil, or other petroleum product is normally inappropriate to

73

use as a charcoal starter since it will give a distinct taste and odor to the food so prepared.

In this case, however, you can get away with it since the overwhelming fishy odor of the river flies will completely mask the odor and taste of the old crankcase oil.

SURPRIZE

urprise! Surprise! This story in the book isn't about river flies at all. It has nothing to do with them. I'm including it in this book, though, because it's a good story and I like it. If you don't like it you'll simply have to put up with it. Besides, I've already gotten your money anyway.

This tale was told to me by my friend, John Gorham who was one of twelve children back on the farm. John has long left the farm, being a photographer and all, now. The scars of being one of a large family back in the thirties and fourties remain, however.

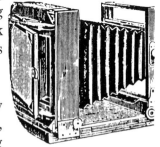

It seems that one day when John was a boy, the family was having some company for supper.

75

Mrs. Gorham found herself caugh a mite shy on groceries, so she took John and his brother Wilber, aside.

"Now, boys, we don't have enough meat for everybody, so when it comes around you two gotta say you don't want any."

With some grumbling, the pair agreed. It was generally understood that it wasn't in a person's best interest to disagree with Mrs. Gorham.

The hour arrived and everybody sat down; that large family plus the company. Things were just as planned. The food was passed, and each helped himself to a nice generous helping of meat. Everybody, that is, except John and Wilber. That forbidden fruit first came to Wilber. He tried not to inhale for fear of getting a whiff of that beautiful roast. He quite casually suggested that he didn't care for any. For one wild moment, he toyed with the idea of spearing a nice hunk of that roast, but he knew better. He could feel his mother's eyes focused right on him. Nonchalantly he passed that plate on to John just as if all it had on it were some carrot sticks.

John glanced idly at the plate and passed it on to yet another brother. Quite coolheaded he was about it all. Not so his stomach. It was frantically yelling to his head to have John drop that nice big piece on the edge off onto his plate. That was to no avail. John had felt the sting of his mother's wrath enough times to know better.

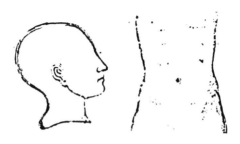

Apparently the boys pulled it off quite well. The meal went without a hitch. Those two boys had some difficulty whipping up a lot of interest in the small talk so typical of mealtime down on the farm. They would have liked to made up for the lack of any meat by wolfing down a mite heavier on the 'taters and gravy. But they didn't. They had been duly warned about that, too.

Soon it was time to clear off the table. Mrs. Gorham quickly did that to make way for the dessert. This hadn't been mentioned, so the boys kind of perked up when they heard their mother getting down those familiar sherbet glasses.

The pair held a whispered conference there at the end of the table, speculating as to what might be forthcoming. The two had spent a long day working on fixin' their father's windmill and they were still hungry.

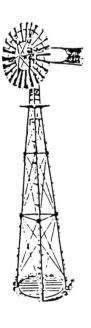

Dessert was always a joyous occasion, but dessert after that meal was nothing less than a Godsend. For what seemed like an eternity, the hungry pair waited for their mother's return.

Sure enough, in a few minutes, Mrs. Gorham came back into the dining room bearing a large tray with a multitude of sherbet glasses, each filled with a strawberry concoction. The boys saw those big beautiful berries fattened against the inside of the glass, all covered with a mound of homemade whipped cream. On top of each scoop of that whipped cream sat another huge berry in solitary splendor. That couldn't have been a more welcome sight to John and Wilber. It was as if everything was all right with the world again.

As Mrs. Gorham returned to the dining room with that treasure, she solved another problem that she hadn't told her sons about. Her problem was that she was a bit shy of dessert, also. Her solution was to enter the room with the following announcement:

"Well, here's some dessert. But anyone who didn't eat their meat doesn't get any."

TECHNIQUE #97

RIVER FLY FLY TIEING

hen Bob Case married the Goodwin girl, the whole Goodwin family was of the firm opinion that little Kathy had really blown it that time. It was abundantly clear that Bob Case was never going to amount to anything. There was endless speculation that "that Case fellow" would never be able to properly provide for Kathy, and that she would not have the comfort of all the necessities and a few of the luxuries of life.

Yes, everyone agreed that the whole thing was a terrible mistake.

It was true that things didn't look just real good for Bob. He was without good training or family contacts.

But, Bob Case had two things going for him. One

was a real sense of ambition, and the other was the river fly. And, it was the river fly that pulled Bob Case's fat right out of the fire.

Bob wasn't what you'd call a real avid fisherman, but he noticed that his friends that were fly fisherman went to great lengths to get their flies tied just right. He heard them complain often

about how the thread and wire would make the flies look so artificial, leaving the fish uninterested in the lure.

Bob reasoned that if he were to build a base fly without any wires or strings he'd have a product that would make him rich ...... rich enough to support Kathy in grand style.

It took a lot of experimenting until Bob figured out how to use those trailin' behind thingies that river flies have to wind around the rest of the critter, all mounted on a fly hook.

But he figured it out, and when he was done, he had the world's only one hundred percent self-tied bass fly.

At first Bob made his all natural tied flies there at his home on the kitchen table.

But the market proved even better than Bob had hoped and he soon built a little machine in his garage to do the whole thing mechanically.

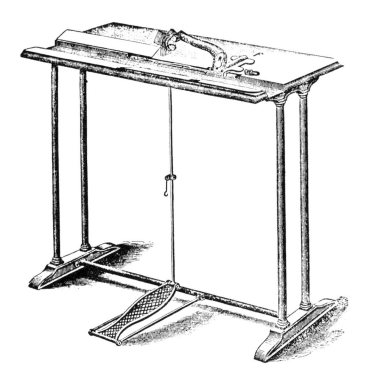

From there it was a natural step to factory in Chicago where tens of thousands of his river fly bass flies were shipped all over the world.

Several of the fancy folks at the wedding of Kathy and Bob who had been telling about how Kathy had blown it were able to get good jobs working for Bob in his fly factory in Chicago.

TECHNIQUE #99

AS A MEANS TO AVOID
EATING NUTRITIOUS FOOD

ne really creative use for river flies was devised by Jesse Lohman from Subula, Iowa.

The fact that Jesse's mother was somewhat less than totally thrilled with river flies was what led the lad to come up with this particular use for our longlegged friends.

Like all boys, Jesse had an adversion to vittles that smacked of being good for him. Those little tidbits of bright orange or yellow that were busting with vitamins, or the mineral laden goodies were, in Jesse's opinion, no match for things like watermelon, rock candy, or sasparilla.

Mrs. Lohman kept a sharp eye on her offspring at dinner time to be sure he didn't sneak food off his plate that he didn't like. Boys have been known to stuff such offending items in their pocket or feed them to the dog when a mother's back was turned, you know.

But, Mrs. Lohman's no-nonsense approach to life in general, and boys eatin' dinner in some particular would go all to pieces when some poor innocent river fly would stumble into the house. When that would happen, everything else would close down until the creature was stomped, swatted, smacked or kicked out.

It didn't take lone for Jesse to take advantage of that situation. He found river flies to be an excellent diversion when it was time to get shed of a hunk of brocolli, a piece of liver, of a blob of "now-eat-this-it's-good-for-you" kind of thing.

All Jesse had to do was to reach to that tiny little ledge up under the table, grab one of his stash of river flies he had there and pitch it up in the air with a "There's one of them River Flies, Ma!!"

Mrs. Lohman's first instinct was to suck in a couple gallons of air and then scream encouragement to everyone in the county to "GET HIM!! GET HIM!!"

Well, Jesse wasn't the kind of kid to let his Ma down. He'd fling a big old hunk of asparagus or slab of liver at that fly in a desperate attempt to bring it down. More than once Jesse nailed the animal right there in midair. 'Course, that's not too difficult when the thing is already dead. But, Mrs. Lohman didn't concern herself with such nicities as the fly bein' alive or dead. She fell for it every time.

TECHNIQUE #100

THE DIVERSION

hen there was Brad Eldon who took a river fly to work with him to hang on the bulletin board.

That poor fly pinned to the corkboard attracted so much attention that folks forsook the normal activities in that office. Those were the watching of each other to see who might be having something going with whom.

Emma Watts, who usually kept a sharp eye on Ted Sooner and the blonde who delivered the mail let her guard down becasue of that dang fly. The two girls in the file room were so upset about the whole thing that they missed noticing if that snotty gal in steno had

her full complement of underthings on or not
that day.

Meanwhile, with all that goin' on, Brad had his
own little secret. He was able to o~~ogl~~.....o~~ggle~~...
..o~~gel~~......watch the girl who was filling in for
Ella Sue for a couple of weeks.

Brad didn't mess around rivers for nuttin'.

TECHNIQUE #101

CHEAP DATES

his technique for using river flies is really for fellows only and is probably best employed after you have successfully gotten a girl friend by means of technique #62 on page 39.

The principle here is to get by with a real cheap date, but simulaneously convince your girl that it is a very romantic and idyllic one.

She need not know that the date is designed to be, and ends up being, simply a cheap one.

What you do is to get to one of those places on the river where they rent power boats that can run you an hourly rental cost approximately six times your hourly wage at work.

The secret is to show utter disdain for those power boats as not being nearly good enough for a date such as yours.

With a wave of your hand, you can quickly pass them by in favor of the more dignified and idyllic rowboat. You want to leave the gal with the impression, of course, that you are going to row her amongst the lilies and the overhanging vines while she idly trails her pinky along, skimming the glass-like water without a care in the world. She needs to be sure to understand that your standards are much too high to subject her to the noise and smell of a greasy old internal combustion engine.

Some judicious selection of the river and where along the shore you choose to go will result in your stirring up a few clouds of river flies. You'll find it doesn't take long for the lady to get her fill of those creepy little things buzzing around and landing on her face and arms.

With a gesture born of pure unadulterated chivalry, you hurriedly thrust the oar/or pole in her hands, explaining that those little creatures will bother less if you keep moving. Gallantly you volunteer to sit there in the boat while she enjoys the advantage of keeping moving necessitated by the rowing or poling.

At this point it helps to kind of guide the boat out into deeper water and away from the shore where most of the flies are. She will quickly notice that fewer flies are bothering her while she enjoys the advantage of doing the work.

It is surprizing, but sometimes you can get away with this three or four times until the gal catches on. And even them, she might as well discover it 'cause if you're sneaky enough to do this, you're sneaky enough to have been doing something else that you'll get caught up on 'bout that time anyway.

But. . . . .

 f any of you folks out there got some more ideas about how to use dead riverflies, you're strongly encouraged not to write and tell me about 'em. I mean, I've done all the thinking about river-flies that I'm gonna do.

So, if you have this urge to pester me about all that, jus' get a second job or take a cold shower or anything 'til the mood passes.

NEED A GIFT?
For

- **Shower** • **Birthday** • **Mother's Day** •
  • **Anniversary** • **Christmas** •

Turn Page For Order Form
(Order NOW While Supply Lasts!)

TO ORDER COPIES OF

101 WAYS TO USE
A DEAD RIVER FLY

Please send me _____ copies of **101 Ways To Use A Dead River Fly** at $7.95 each. (Make checks payable to **QUIXOTE PRESS.**)

Name _____

Street _____

City _____ State_____ Zip Code_____

SEND ORDER TO:
QUIXOTE PRESS
R.R. #4, Box 33B
Blvd. Station
Sioux City, Iowa 51109

TO ORDER COPIES OF

101 WAYS TO USE
A DEAD RIVER FLY

Please send me _____ copies of **101 Ways To Use A Dead River Fly** at $7.95 each. (Make checks payable to **QUIXOTE PRESS.**)

Name _____

Street _____

City _____ State_____ Zip Code_____

SEND ORDER TO:
QUIXOTE PRESS
R.R. #4, Box 33B
Blvd. Station
Sioux City, Iowa 51109

INDEX

Index

.........Oh, what the heck. You don't really need an index for this book. Compiling an index can really be a pain in the neck and I'm not sure I'm up to it this morning.

Thanks for buying this book!

*If you have enjoyed this book, perhaps you
would enjoy others from Quixote Press.*

GHOSTS OF THE MISSISSIPPI RIVER
Mpls. to Dubuque by Bruce Carlson . . . . paperback $9.95

GHOSTS OF THE MISSISSIPPI RIVER
Dubuque to Keokuk by Bruce Carlson . . . . paperback $9.95

GHOSTS OF THE MISSISSIPPI RIVER
Keokuk to St. Louis by Bruce Carlson . . . . paperback $9.95

HOW TO TALK MIDWESTERN
by Robert Thomas . . . . paperback $7.95

GHOSTS OF DES MOINES COUNTY, IOWA
by Bruce Carlson . . . . hardback $12.00

GHOSTS OF SCOTT COUNTY, IOWA
by Bruce Carlson . . . . hardback $12.95

GHOSTS OF ROCK ISLAND COUNTY, ILLINOIS
by Bruce Carlson . . . . hardback $12.95

GHOSTS OF THE AMANA COLONIES
by Lori Erickson . . . . paperback $9.95

GHOSTS OF NORTHEAST IOWA
by Ruth Hein and Vicky Hinsenbrock . . . . paperback $9.95

GHOSTS OF POLK COUNTY, IOWA
by Tom Welch . . . . paperback $9.95

GHOSTS OF THE IOWA GREAT LAKES
by Bruce Carlson . . . . paperback $9.95

MEMOIRS OF A DAKOTA HUNTER
by Gary Scholl . . . . paperback $9.95

LOST AND BURIED TREASURE ALONG
THE MISSISSIPPI
by Gary Scholl and Netha Bell . . . . paperback $9.95
(Continued on Next Page)

MISSISSIPPI RIVER PO' FOLK
by Pat Wallace . . . . .paperback $9.95

STRANGE FOLKS ALONG THE MISSISSIPPI
by Pat Wallace . . . . .paperback $9.95

THE VANISHING OUTHOUSE OF IOWA
by Bruce Carlson . . . . .paperback $9.95

THE VANISHING OUTHOUSE OF ILLINOIS
by Bruce Carlson . . . . .paperback $9.95

THE VANISHING OUTHOUSE OF MINNESOTA
by Bruce Carlson . . . . .paperback $9.95

THE VANISHING OUTHOUSE OF WISCONSIN
by Bruce Carlson . . . . .paperback $9.95

MISSISSIPPI RIVER COOKIN' BOOK
by Bruce Carlson . . . . .paperback $11.95

IOWA'S ROAD KILL COOKBOOK
by Bruce Carlson . . . . .paperback $7.95

HITCH HIKING THE UPPER MIDWEST
by Bruce Carlson . . . . .paperback $7.95

IOWA, THE LAND BETWEEN THE VOWELS
by Bruce Carlson . . . . .paperback $9.95
(Farm Boy Stories From the Early 1900's)

GHOSTS OF SOUTHWEST MINNESOTA
by Ruth Hein . . . . .paperback $9.95

ME 'N WESLEY
by Bruce Carlson . . . . .paperback $9.95
*(Stories about the homemade toys that farm children made
and played with around the turn of the century.)*

SOUTH DAKOTA ROAD KILL COOKBOOK
by Bruce Carlson . . . . .paperback $7.95

(Continued on Next Page)

GHOSTS OF THE BLACK HILLS
by Tom Welch...........................paperback $9.95

Some Pretty Tame, But Kinda Funny Stories About Early DAKOTA LADIES-OF-THE-EVENING
by Bruce Carlson ....paperback $9.95

Some Pretty Tame, But Kinda Funny Stories About Early IOWA LADIES-OF-THE-EVENING
by Bruce Carlson ....paperback $9.95

Some Pretty Tame, But Kinda Funny Stories About Early ILLINOIS LADIES-OF-THE-EVENING
by Bruce Carlson ....paperback $9.95

Some Pretty Tame, But Kinda Funny Stories About Early MINNESOTA LADIES-OF-THE-EVENING
by Bruce Carlson ....paperback $9.95

Some Pretty Tame, But Kinda Funny Stories About Early WISCONSIN LADIES-OF-THE-EVENING
by Bruce Carlson ....paperback $9.95

Some Pretty Tame, But Kinda Funny Stories About Early MISSOURI LADIES-OF-THE-EVENING
by Bruce Carlson ....paperback $9.95

THE DAKOTA'S VANISHING OUTHOUSE
by Bruce Carlson ....paperback $9.95

ILLINOIS' ROAD KILL COOKBOOK
by Bruce Carlson ....paperback $7.95

OLD IOWA HOUSES, YOUNG LOVES
by Bruce Carlson ....paperback $9.95
*(Stories about old houses in Iowa
and young loves they have known.)*

TERROR IN THE BLACK HILLS
by Dick Kennedy ....paperback $9.95

IOWA'S EARLY HOME REMEDIES
by various ....paperback $9.95

GHOSTS OF DOOR COUNTY, WISCONSIN
by Geri Rider ....paperback $9.95

THE VANISHING OUTHOUSE OF MISSOURI
by Bruce Carlson ....paperback $9.95

JACK KING vs. DETECTIVE Mac KENZIE
by N. Bell ....paperback $9.95

RIVER SHARKS & SHENANIGANS
(tales of riverboat gambling of years ago)
by N. Bell ....paperback $9.95

TALES OF HACKETT'S CREEK
(1940s Mississippi River Kids)
by D. Titus ....paperback $9.95

LOST & BURIED TREASURE OF THE MISSISSIPPI RIVER
by N. Bell ....paperback $9.95

ROMANCE ON BOARD
by Helen Colby...........................paperback $9.95

UNSOLVED MYSTERIES OF THE MISSISSIPPI
by N. Bell ....paperback $9.95

TALL TALES OF THE MISSISSIPPI RIVER
by D. Titus ....paperback $9.95

TALL TALES OF THE MISSOURI RIVER
by D. Titus ....paperback $9.95

MAKIN' DO IN SOUTH DAKOTA
by various ....paperback $9.95

TRICKS WE PLAYED IN IOWA
by various ....paperback $9.95

CHILDREN OF THE RIVER
by various . . . . paperback $9.95

LET'S GO DOWN TO THE RIVER 'AN. . . .
by various . . . . paperback $9.95

EARLY WISCONSIN HOME REMEDIES
by various . . . . paperback $9.95

EARLY MISSOURI HOME REMEDIES
by various . . . . paperback $9.95

MY VERY FIRST. . . .
by various . . . . paperback $9.95

101 WAYS FOR IOWANS TO DO IN THEIR NEIGHBOR'S PESKY DOG WITHOUT GETTING CAUGHT
by B. Carlson . . . . paperback $7.95

SOUTH DAKOTA ROADKILL COOKBOOK
by B. Carlson . . . . paperback $7.95

A FIELD GUIDE TO IOWA'S CRITTERS
by B. Carlson . . . . paperback $7.95

A FIELD GUIDE TO MISSOURI'S CRITTERS
by B. Carlson . . . . paperback $7.95

MISSOURI'S ROADKILL COOKBOOK
by B. Carlson . . . . paperback $7.95

A FIELD GUIDE TO ILLINOIS' CRITTERS
by B. Carlson . . . . paperback $7.95

MINNESOTA'S ROADKILL COOKBOOK
by B. Carlson . . . . paperback $7.95

REVENGE OF THE ROADKILL
by B. Carlson . . . . paperback $7.95

THE MOTORIST'S FIELD GUIDE TO MIDWEST FARM EQUIPMENT
(misguided information as only a city
slicker can get it messed up)
by B. Carlson ....paperback $7.95

ILLINOIS EARLY HOME REMEDIES
by various ....paperback $9.95

GUNSHOOTIN', WHISKEY DRINKIN', GIRL CHASIN' TALES OUT OF THE OLD DAKOTA TERRITORY
by Netha Bell ....paperback $9.95

WYOMING'S ROADKILL COOKBOOK
by B. Carlson ....paperback $7.95

MONTANA'S ROADKILL COOKBOOK
by B. Carlson ....paperback $7.95

SHE CRIED WITH HER BOOTS ON
(tales of an early Nebraska housewife)
by M. Walsh ....paperback $9.95

SKUNK RIVER ANTHOLOGY
by Gene "Will" Olson ....paperback $9.95

101 WAYS TO USE A DEAD RIVER FLY
by B. Carlson ....paperback $7.95